Guidance for Health Care Joint Ventures:

A Comparison of the Requirements of the Antitrust, Fraud and Abuse, and Self-Referral Laws

Peter M. Kazon
O'Connor & Hannan
Washington, D.C.

AN ASPEN PUBLICATION

GUIDANCE FOR HEALTH CARE JOINT VENTURES

Table of Contents **Page**

In one recent antitrust case involving a dispute between competing HMOs, Judge Boudin of the First Circuit stated, "In simpler days, health care comprised a doctor, a patient and sometimes a hospital, but the Norman Rockwell era of medicine has given way to a new world of diverse and complex insurance and provider arrangements."[1] Today, the press is full of reports of health care providers forming novel types of arrangements for the purpose of furnishing health care services. Such arrangements may involve hospitals, or groups of physicians, or both, that combine to form an entity that offers some new health care item or service.

There are a variety of legal issues created whenever a health care joint venture is established, because both the federal antitrust and the Medicare fraud and abuse laws are implicated. In addition, similar state laws and federal and state tax laws must also be considered.[2]

These issues become even more complicated when the joint venture is formed by health care providers who will also do business with the entity. For example, a group of internists may establish a laboratory, or a diagnostic imaging center, to which they also refer their patients. In other instances, a hospital may establish a durable medical equipment (DME) provider to which patients in need of equipment are referred, or a hospital may contract with a provider of ambulance services for its patients needing these services. In still other situations, a hospital and physicians on its staff may establish a venture together. As reform of the health care system progresses, and providers further integrate their operations, all of these arrangements are likely to become even more common.

Some commentators have suggested that when the health care provider can profit from his or her referrals, such "ancillary service joint ventures" may create a conflict-of-interest.[3] In addition, research has suggested that "self-referral," the practice by which providers refer patients to an entity in which they have an interest, may give providers an incentive to increase their utilization of the

1. *U.S. Healthcare Inc. v. Healthsource, Inc.*, 986 F.2d 589, 591 (1st Cir. 1993).

2. For the most part, these tax and state law issues are beyond the scope of this article and will not be discussed.

3. *See, e.g.*, Arnold S. Relman, M.D., *The New Medical-Industrial Complex*, 303 New Eng. J. of Med. 963 (1980); Arnold S. Relman, M.D., *The Shattuck Lecture—The Health Care Industry: Where is it Taking Us?* 325 New Eng. J. of Med. 855 (1991). In fact, the American Medical Association, after changing its position several times, now takes the position that in most instances it is a violation of ethical standards for physicians to refer patients to a health facility outside of the physician's office practice at which he or she does not provide direct patient care, when the physician has an investment interest in that facility. *See* AMA Council on Ethical and Judicial Affairs, *Code of Medical Ethics, Current Opinions with Annotations*, 102-03 (1994).

services offered by the venture, thereby leading to higher health care costs.[4] As a result of such studies, Congress has enacted legislation specifically directed at the phenomenon of self-referral and may expand that law as a result of health care reform legislation now being considered.

The purpose of this article is to give some guidance concerning the various legal considerations that arise in the formation and operation of a health care joint venture, especially when the health care providers who refer to it or use its services also have financial arrangements with the entity. We begin with a discussion of the background of the antitrust laws, the fraud and abuse laws, and the self-referral laws as they relate to this topic. Then, we will turn to a fuller discussion of the specific issues that can arise in the formation and operation of such joint ventures.

I. BACKGROUND OF THE APPLICABLE LAWS

A. The Antitrust Laws

In analyzing health care joint ventures, the Federal Trade Commission ("FTC") and the U.S. Department of Justice—the two antitrust enforcement agencies—make use of two types of antitrust analysis. Some practices are considered "inherently suspect," that is, they are considered the kind of activity that is likely to reduce competition and restrict output. These types of practices are termed "*per se*" illegal. Once the existence of such an arrangement is shown, it is no defense to argue that the arrangement did not have an adverse effect on competition. For example, because price-fixing is *per se* illegal, the parties to the arrangement cannot argue in defense that they set prices at a reasonable level.[5]

Arrangements that are not *per se* illegal are judged under the "rule of reason." This analysis balances the procompetitive aspects of the arrangement against the anticompetitive aspects to determine the overall or "net" effect on competition.

4. *See, e.g.*, Jean Mitchell, *et al.*, *Consequences of Physicians' Ownership of Health Care Facilities—Joint Ventures in Radiation Therapy*, 327 New Eng. J. of Med. 1497 (1992); Alex Swedlow, *et al.*, *Increased Costs and Rates of Use in California Workers' Compensation System as a Result of Self-Referral by Physicians*, 327 New Eng. J. of Med. 1502 (1992); Bruce Hillman, *et al.*, *Physicians' Utilization and Charges for Outpatient Diagnostic Imaging in a Medicare Population*, 268 J.A.M.A. 2050 (1992); Jean Mitchell, *et al.*. *Physician Ownership of Physical Therapy Services*, 268 J.A.M.A. 2055 (1992); State of Florida Health Care Cost Containment Board, *Joint Ventures Among Health Care Providers in Florida* (1991); Office of Inspector General, Dept. of Health and Human Services, *Financial Arrangements Between Physicians and Health Care Businesses*, (Rept. No. OAI-12-88-1410) (May, 1989).

5. *See, e.g.*, *Arizona v. Maricopa County Medical Society*, 457 U.S. 332 (1982).

Under the rule of reason, courts and antitrust authorities conduct a much fuller analysis of the markets involved, the nature of the competition, and the purpose of the arrangement.[6]

Thus, in structuring a joint venture, it is important to avoid provisions that could result in *per se* condemnation. Rather, the venture should be structured so that it will be analyzed under the rule of reason, should an antitrust issue arise.[7] In the course of this article, we will discuss the types of provisions that can give rise to such *per se* liability and those that will be analyzed under the rule of reason.

Until recently, the antitrust enforcement agencies viewed ancillary service joint ventures as a form of vertical integration; thus, such arrangements were considered unlikely to be anticompetitive. For example, when the FTC commented on a "Notice of Intent" issued by the HHS Office of Inspector General ("OIG") concerning physician investment in ancillary service joint ventures, it noted such investment could be procompetitive because the investing physicians may have recognized a particular need in their community or may have invested to assure continued high quality of care at the facility.[8] Interestingly, however, in the 1970s, the FTC staff had recommended a full investigation of the problem of physician self-referral with a view towards a formal rulemaking on the issue, although it does not appear such an investigation was ever pursued.[9]

Recently, however, the FTC has expressed greater interest in this area. On January 30, 1992, Kevin J. Arquit, then-Director of the FTC's Bureau of Competition spoke before the National Health Lawyers Association and addressed the subject of physician investment in ancillary service joint ventures.[10] In his speech, Mr. Arquit noted:

6. *See, e.g., NCAA v. Board of Reagents of Univ. of Okla.*, 468 U.S. 85 (1984).

7. For a general analysis of the antitrust issues raised by health care joint ventures, *see* K. Grady, *A Framework for Antitrust Analysis of Health Care Joint Ventures*, 61 Antitrust L.J. 765 (1993); J. Miles, *Health Care & Antitrust Law* at 13-5 to 13-7 (1992).

8. *See Comments of the FTC Concerning the Development of Regulations Pursuant to the Medicare and Medicaid Anti-Kickback Statute*, submitted to the Department of HHS (December 18, 1987) (LRR-17-NI).

9. An FTC staff memorandum discussing this issue was obtained by the National Association of Retail Druggists under the Freedom of Information Act. It is reprinted in the record of Congressional hearings held on self-referral. *Hearings on H.R. 939 Before the Subcomm. on Health and the Subcomm. on Oversight of the House Ways and Means Comm.*, 101st Cong., 1st Sess. at 279 (1989).

10. Kevin J. Arquit, "A New Concern in Health Care Antitrust Enforcement: Acquisition and Exercise of Market Power by Physician Ancillary Joint Ventures" (Jan. 30, 1992) (hereinafter "*Arquit Speech*"). *See also* Commissioner Deborah K. Owen, "Antitrust Enforcement and the Health Care Crisis," remarks before the American Bar Association Section of Antitrust Law (Jan. 21, 1992).

> [T]he same physician-owner incentives for self-referral that lie at the heart of the conflict-of-interest issue may give rise to antitrust concerns: the potential in some cases for creating or enhancing market power in markets for the ancillary goods or services resulting in higher prices and lower quality health care to consumers and monopoly profits to some health care suppliers.[11]

The essential antitrust problem created by such arrangements was further explained by another FTC official, Mark Horoschak, Assistant Director for Health Care in the FTC's Bureau of Competition. In an article, he noted:

> If a sufficiently high proportion of the physicians participate in the joint venture, the aggregation of their practices may effectively create market power for the venture with respect to the provision of the ancillary service, because the ownership interest creates a strong incentive for physician-owners to channel their patients to the joint venture. Thus, it would appear that the arrangement itself could effectively force existing competitors out of the market and foreclose others from entering the market and selling to these patients. Simply put, the combination of physicians allows the joint venture to attain and maintain a dominant share of the market for the ancillary service, other than through competition on the merits.[12]

In his article, Mr. Horoschak suggests that such a venture could be attacked under three separate theories. First, it could be attacked under section 2 of the Sherman Act, because it could give rise to monopolization of the service offered by the joint venture. Second, the joint venture could be vulnerable under Section 7 of the Clayton Act, if the investors acquired the shares or assets of a single enterprise and the acquisition appeared likely to substantially lessen competition or tended to create a monopoly. Finally, the arrangement could be unlawful under Section 1 of the Sherman Act, if the requisite agreement to restrain trade could be shown. In that instance, the arrangement would likely be analyzed under the rule of reason, to determine the possible competitive effects.[13]

Recently, the FTC accepted a series of consent agreements involving self-referral issues with two home medical equipment firms and their 28 physician investors. In these cases, the FTC alleged that the physician-owners of the ventures included about 60 percent of the pulmonologists who were the likely referrors for the home oxygen services supplied by the venture. As a result, the

11. *Arquit Speech*, at 11.

12. *See* Mark J. Horoschak, *Antitrust Perspectives On Joint Ventures Among Health Care Providers*, 6 Antitrust Health Care Chronicle 2 (1992) (hereinafter "*Horoschak*"). Mr. Horoschak is Assistant Director for Health Care in the FTC's Bureau of Competition.

13. *Id.*

doctors allegedly were able to control access to home oxygen systems and create barriers to entry by new entities.[14]

B. The Fraud and Abuse Laws

The second body of law that must be considered in the formation and operation of these joint ventures are the fraud and abuse laws, which are enforced by the Office of Inspector General of the Department of Health and Human Services ("OIG"). The principal federal fraud and abuse statute is Section 1128B of the Social Security Act.[15] The first section of the law, Section 1128B(a), prohibits providers from making false statements or representations in connection with claims reimbursed by the Medicare or Medicaid programs, and thereby obtaining money from these programs to which the provider is not entitled.[16] The second section of the law, Section 1128B(b), is the provision that is of particular concern to this discussion.[17] This law prohibits the offering or payment, or the solicitation or acceptance, of "any remuneration (including any kickback, bribe or rebate), directly or indirectly, overtly or covertly, in cash or in kind" in exchange for the referral of a patient for items or services reimbursed by Medicare or Medicaid.[18]

Certain types of payment are specifically excluded from the definition of "remuneration," included in the antikickback law. There are exceptions set out in the law for discounts that are reported and passed on to Medicare or Medicaid; for amounts paid to employees by employers as compensation; for payments by certain group purchasing organizations; and for payments permitted by federal "safe harbor" regulations. Several of these exceptions are discussed at greater length below. Violation of Section 1128B(b) is a felony punishable by a fine of

14. In re: Home Oxygen & Medical Equipment Co., FTC, File No. 901-0109; In re: Certain Home Oxygen Pulmonologists, FTC, File No. 901-0109; In re: Homecare Oxygen & Medical Co., FTC, File No. 911-0020, 58 Fed. Reg. 60653 (Nov. 17, 1993) [hereinafter "Home Oxygen"].

In September, 1993, the FTC and the Department of Justice also issued a set of policy statements, "Statements of Antitrust Enforcement Policy in the Health Care Area," but these do not specifically discuss investment by physicians in entities supplying ancillary services, to which the physicians also refer patients. *See* 4 Trade Reg. Rep. (CCH) ¶13,150 (1993) [hereinafter "Policy Statements"].

15. 42 U.S.C. §1320a-7b.

16. 42 U.S.C. §1320a-7b(a). Federal enforcement agencies also utilize other statutes, such as the federal False Claims Act, to pursue similar claims.

17. 42 U.S.C. §1320a-7b(b).

18. *Id.* It should be noted that many states have their own antikickback laws, which are not limited to items and services reimbursed by Medicare and Medicaid. In addition, several of the health care reform bills being considered by Congress would expand the application of Section 1128B to cover services paid for by private payors.

up to $25,000 or imprisonment or both. In addition, the government may seek to exclude the provider from the Medicare and Medicaid programs.[19]

In using the word "remuneration" in the antikickback law, Congress purposely chose a word that would have very broad applicability, and courts have condemned a broad range of activities under the antikickback law. For example, in a seminal case, *United States v. Greber*,[20] the court examined payments to physicians made by a medical diagnostic company providing holter monitor services. The company billed Medicare for the services provided and forwarded 40 percent of the amount it received to the referring physician. Although the defendant alleged these payments were legitimate "interpretation fees," the Third Circuit declined to examine whether a legitimate purpose would excuse such payments. It concluded, "if one purpose of the payment is to induce referrals, the Medicare statute has been violated."[21] Other cases have adopted the *Greber* reasoning.[22]

For the purpose of most health care joint ventures, the key issue is whether a dividend or other return on investment paid to an investor who also refers to the entity will be considered "remuneration," and, thus, an unlawful kickback. The one case that specifically applied the antikickback law to a joint venture situation is *OIG v. Hanlester Network*. In that case, the OIG charged the principals of the Hanlester Network, a group of physician-owned laboratories, with violations of the antikickback law.

The OIG sued three limited partnerships, each of which owned a laboratory in California, and sought to exclude the principals from the Medicare program on the grounds that the dividends earned by the physician-investors constituted "remuneration" and thus violated the antikickback law. The case has had a long and complex procedural history. The first Administrative Law Judge ("ALJ") decision was reversed by the HHS Departmental Appeals Board ("DAB"), because it determined that the ALJ had incorrectly required proof of an explicit

19. Soc. Sec. Act, §1128(b)(7); 42 U.S.C. §1320-7(b)(7). Unlike the antitrust laws, there is no private right of action under the antikickback law. *See Action Ambulance Serv. Inc. v. Atlanticare Health Serv.*, 815 F.Supp. 33, 37 (D. Mass. 1993). *See also American Health Syst. Inc. v. Visiting Nurses Ass'n.*, 1994-1 Trade Cas. (CCH) ¶70,633 (E.D. Pa. 1994) (permitting RICO action based on antikickback violations). Several of the health care reform bills being considered by Congress would also permit private payors, insurance companies, to bring their own claims for violations of the fraud and abuse laws.

20. 760 F.2d 68 (3rd Cir.), *cert. denied*, 474 U.S. 988 (1985).

21. *Id.* at 69.

22. *See United States v. Bay State Ambulance and Hosp. Rental Service, Inc.*, 874 F.2d 20 (1st Cir. 1989); *United States v. Kats*, 871 F.2d 105 (9th Cir. 1989).

agreement to refer patients to the joint venture.[23] On remand, the ALJ found a violation of the statute and excluded some, but not all, of the respondents.[24] On appeal, the DAB affirmed the finding of violation but found that all the respondents should be excluded.[25] That decision was upheld by a U.S. District Court in California and is now on appeal to the Ninth Circuit.[26]

In *Hanlester*, the OIG alleged that the physician-investors were told that they would be the initial sources of the laboratories' business and that physicians who regularly ordered such tests would be sought as investors. Physician-investors were also allegedly warned that it would be "a blueprint for failure" if partners in the venture did not refer. One sales representative working for the network reportedly told prospective investors that they could expect to earn annual returns of three to four hundred percent; that their investments were virtually guaranteed; that the number of shares that any one investor could buy would be tied to the volume of referrals that were anticipated from that physician; and that any limited partner who did not refer would be pressured to sell back his or her interest.[27]

In its decision to remand to the ALJ, the DAB noted for a violation of the antikickback law to occur, all that was required was that the payments be made to induce referrals. It defined "to induce" as "an intent to exercise influence over reason or judgment in an effort to cause a desired action..."[28] It went on to state: "Thus, in the ownership setting, an illegal inducement may consist of an opportunity to earn money on the investment, if a non-incidental purpose of providing that opportunity is to induce referrals."[29] The Board found that such a determination could only be made after an evaluation of all the circumstances surrounding the transaction.[30]

The DAB said, however, that in making a decision on remand, the ALJ could consider the following as evidence that the payments were made as an inducement:

23. *Inspector General v. Hanlester Network*, [1991 Transfer Binder] Medicare & Medicaid Guide (CCH) ¶39,094 (1991) (ALJ decision); [1992-1 Transfer Binder] Medicare & Medicaid Guide (CCH) ¶39,566 (1991) (Departmental Appeals Board decision reversing ALJ and remanding the case).

24. [1992-2 Transfer Binder] Medicare & Medicaid Guide (CCH) ¶40,064 (1992).

25. [1992-2 Transfer Binder] Medicare & Medicaid Guide (CCH) ¶40,406B (1992).

26. [1993-1 Transfer Binder] Medicare & Medicaid Guide (CCH) ¶41,076 (1993).

27. *See* [1992-1 Transfer Binder] Medicare & Medicaid Guide at 27,742.

28. *Id.* at 27,747.

29. *Id.* at 27,755.

30. *Id.* at 27,762.

- that payments were in excess of the value of the services provided or the investment made;
- that the return on the investment was excessive in terms of the risks involved or the return available on alternative investments;
- that the opportunity to invest was available only to potential referrors;
- that investors were discouraged from using other laboratories;
- that payments were in some way proportional to a physician's referrals;
- that the remuneration offered was sufficient to interfere with the physician's judgment based on legitimate considerations, such as cost, quality and necessity of services[31]

In addition to the cases discussed above, there are several other sources for the interpretation of the antikickback law as it applies to ancillary service joint ventures. In 1989, the OIG issued a "Fraud Alert" to all Medicare providers, which stated that the OIG was aware of a number of "joint ventures" formed between those in a position to refer business, such as physicians, and those providing items or services for which Medicare or Medicaid would pay. The OIG noted that in many instances, the purpose of the ventures was not to raise capital, "but to lock up a stream of referrals from the physician investors and to compensate them indirectly for these referrals."

The Fraud Alert identified the indicia of such suspicious joint ventures by focusing on three areas. It looked first to the manner in which investors were selected; *i.e.*, were investors chosen simply because they were in a position to make referrals? Second, it examined the structure of the venture; *i.e.*, was the joint venture a legitimate entity or merely a shell that simply billed for work performed somewhere else? Third, it considered the financing of the venture and its profit distributions; *i.e.*, were investors receiving large returns on a relatively small investment, which carried little risk? As we shall see below, these three areas are a useful framework of analysis for the issues presented by such joint ventures.

The basic principles outlined in the Fraud Alert were amplified considerably in the "safe harbor" regulations issued by the OIG. Because the antikickback statute is so broad, in 1987, Congress required the OIG to promulgate regulations that would identify those practices that would be immune from prosecution under the law, even though the conduct might come within the literal terms of the statute. On July 29, 1991, the OIG issued the first set of safe harbor regulations.[32]

31. *Id.* at 27,763.

32. 56 Fed. Reg. 35951 (1991). The safe harbor regulations are now codified in 42 C.F.R. §1001.95; however, some clarifications to these regulations were proposed by the OIG in July, 1994. *See* 59 Fed. Reg. 37203 (July 21, 1994).

These safe harbor regulations define a number of different practices that will be immune from prosecution under the federal antikickback law. Conduct meeting the requirements of the regulations is immunized; conduct outside the requirements of the regulations is not illegal, it simply will not be exempt from prosecution.[33]

The safe harbors cover the following areas: investment interests; space and equipment rentals; personal service/management contracts; sale of practice; referral services; warranties; waiver of deductible for hospital care; discounts; payments to employees; and payments by group purchasing organizations. The OIG issued two additional sets of safe harbor regulations covering managed care entities and miscellaneous other issues.[34]

For purposes of our analysis, it is the investment safe harbor that is the most important. This safe harbor applies to investments in two different types of entities: large, publicly-traded entities and smaller entities, such as limited partnerships. To qualify for the "publicly-traded entity" safe harbor, the entity must have possessed more than $50 million in "undepreciated net tangible assets" during the previous fiscal year or previous 12-month period, and must meet the following requirements:

1. Any equity security in the entity must be registered with the SEC;
2. The investment interest of an investor who refers to the entity or generates business for the entity must be obtained on terms equally available to the public through trading on a national securities exchange;
3. The entity or investors must not market or furnish the entity's services to partners or shareholders differently than to non-investors;
4. The entity must not loan funds or guarantee a loan for an investor who refers or does business with the entity, if the investor uses any part of the loan to obtain the investment interest; and
5. The return on investment must be directly proportional to the amount of the capital investment of that investor.[35]

It is the safe harbor for small entities, however, that is likely to be of the greatest interest to most ancillary service joint ventures. The safe harbor establishes eight requirements that must be met for immunity to apply and these requirements must be met by all the investors in the entity. For purposes of this regulation, "investors" are classified as either "passive" or "active." An active investor includes a *bona fide* general partner or an individual or an entity that agrees in writing to undertake liability for the entity's agents. "Passive investors"

33. 56 Fed. Reg. at 35954.
34. 57 Fed. Reg. at 52,723 (Nov. 5, 1992); 58 Fed. Reg. at 49008 (Sept. 21, 1993).
35. 42 C.F.R. §1001.952(a)(1). *See also* 59 Fed. Reg. at 37203-04.

are those investors who are not active investors, including limited partners and shareholders. Unless otherwise noted, all investors must meet the safe harbor requirements; thus, if the active investors qualify, but the passive investors do not, or vice versa, then none of the investors will receive safe harbor status.[36]

It is important to note that the antikickback law and the safe harbor regulations are only implicated if the services are reimbursed by Medicare or Medicaid. If the entity does not accept Medicare and Medicaid patients, then the law and the regulations do not apply.[37] Of course, state antikickback law might still be relevant.

The specific requirements of the safe harbors will be discussed in greater detail below. At this point, it is important to emphasize that the requirements fall into the same three areas that were used in the Fraud Alert, discussed above: (1) the manner in which investors are selected and retained; (2) the nature of the business structure; and (3) the financing and profit distributions of the venture.

C. The Self-Referral Law

As a result of studies on the effects of self-referral, increasing attention has also been given to this issue by Congress. In 1989, Congressman Pete Stark (D-CA) introduced, and Congress passed, one of the first self-referral laws. Under this provision, beginning in 1992, if a physician had a financial relationship with an entity providing clinical laboratory services, then the physician was prohibited from referring his or her Medicare patients' testing to that entity, unless one of the exceptions in the statute applied. In addition, the entity was prohibited from billing for those services.[38]

In the 1993 budget bill, the Omnibus Budget Reconciliation Act of 1993 ("OBRA '93"), Congress amended the self-referral law to clarify some of the exceptions and extended the services covered by the self-referral prohibition. As a result of these changes, beginning in 1995, it will be unlawful for a physician to refer Medicare or Medicaid patients for the services set out below, if he or she has a financial relationship with the entity furnishing the services. The services covered by the new prohibition are: clinical laboratory services; physical therapy services; occupational therapy services; radiology or other diagnostic services; radiation therapy services; durable medical equipment; parenteral and enteral nutrients, equipment, and supplies; prosthetics, orthotics, and prosthetic devices; home health services; outpatient prescription drugs; and inpatient and

36. 42 C.F.R. §1001.952(a)(2).
37. *See* 56 Fed. Reg. at 35,954.
38. *See* Soc. Sec. Act, §1877; 42 U.S.C. §1395nn.

outpatient hosptial services.[39] In addition, several of the health reform bills currently being considered in Congress would amend the law still further. The version passed by the House Ways and Means Committee would apply the self-referral prohibition to referrals reimbursed by private payors, in addition to those reimbursed by Medicare and Medicaid.

The self-referral law applies to an ownership or investment interest in an entity held by a physician or immediate family member and to a "compensation arrangement" between the physician (or immediate family member) and the entity. A compensation arrangement arises whenever some form of remuneration flows, in either direction, between the referring physician and the entity. Thus, if a compensation arrangement exists, the physician would not be able to make referrals to that entity unless an exception applied. There are a number of specific exceptions to both the investment and the compensation arrangement provisions, however, set out in the law. The law also requires entities to file a disclosure form listing their investors and those physicians with whom the entity has compensation arrangements.

It is important to emphasize that the self-referral law is totally distinct from the antikickback law. Thus, compliance with a safe harbor does *not* relieve a health care provider of complying with the self-referral law.[40] Similarly, compliance with the requirements of one of the exceptions in the self-referral law does not mean one is immune from prosecution under the antikickback law.[41]

In addition, it is important to bear in mind that many individual states, have now also passed their own self-referral laws. In many instances, these are broader than the federal law. With this background, we can now turn to the more specific guidelines.

II. GUIDELINES FOR THE FORMATION OF JOINT VENTURES

Having sketched the legal background, we can now turn to some guidelines for establishing health care ventures. In a general sense, there are issues that arise both in the structuring and in the operation of joint ventures. As noted above, the structural issues can be easily divided into the three areas considered by the OIG in the Fraud Alert and the safe harbor regulations: the selection and retention of participants; the actual structure of the venture; and, the financing and profit distributions of the venture. In discussing the operation of the venture, we will focus on several additional issues: "channeling" patients to the venture; discour-

39. OBRA '93, Pub. L. No. 103-66, 107 Stat. 596 (1993) [hereinafter "OBRA '93"].

40. *See* 56 Fed. Reg. at 35957.

41. *See* 57 Fed. Reg. 8588, 8593 (Mar. 11, 1992) (HCFA proposed regulations to implement Section 1877).

aging referrors from using competing providers; and pricing the services of the venture. In each instance below, we will first address the antitrust issues, then the fraud and abuse issues, and, finally, the self-referral issues.

A. Selection of Participants

1. *The Antitrust Issues*

The first question faced by almost any venture will be: who should be allowed to invest in the venture? As noted above, antitrust concern will be raised if such a large proportion of the providers in an area participated that they could exercise market power and prevent new entry. As noted above, because an ownership interest may give a physician an incentive to channel patients to the venture, if a large percentage of the potential referrors were involved in the entity, competitors could be forced out of the market and new entry could be discouraged. Thus, the first issue will be to ensure that the venture does not include too large a proportion of potential referrors.

There is no hard-and-fast rule concerning what percentage of physicians would raise concerns. In analyzing provider-controlled PPOs, the Department of Justice used, at one time, a 35 percent "safe harbor;" that is, the Department would not attack a venture if the percentage of physicians involved was less than 35 percent. However, under former Assistant Attorney General James F. Rill, the Department gave up this "bright line" test in favor of a "richer analysis" based on the Department's Merger Guidelines.[42] In their Policy Statements, the FTC and the Department of Justice stated they would not attack a physician PPO arrangement if the venture consisted of less than 20 percent of the physicians in a particular market, if other conditions were met.[43]

In the *Home Oxygen* cases, the FTC required enough of the physicians involved to divest their interest, so that no more than 25 percent of the pulmonologists practicing in the area were members of the venture. The consent order specificially notes that the 25 percent figure was selected to prevent the companies from maintaining a captive source of referrals large enough to confer market power and to afford some "fencing-in relief" to prevent similar problems in the future.[44] Thus, 20-25 percent is probably a useful benchmark so long as there are not other factors limiting entry or affecting competition.

42. James F. Rill, "Antitrust Enforcement Policy and the Treatment of Horizontal Price Restraints: Lessons for the Health Care Industry," remarks to the National Health Lawyers Association (Feb. 15, 1991) (hereinafter "*Rill Speech*").

43. 4 Trade Reg. Rep. (CCH) ¶13,150 at 20764-65.

44. *See* 58 Fed. Reg. at 60659.

In calculating this market share, however, it will be important to remember who the likely referrors are. If a particular type of specialist is the most likely referror, then it will be necessary to determine what percentage of those specialists are involved. For example, as nephrologists are the likely referrors for patients in need of dialysis services, a venture that was composed of a large percentage of the nephrologists in an area could raise antitrust issues, because presumably they would be unlikely to refer to a new dialysis provider that entered the market.[45] In the *Home Oxygen* cases, the concern was that the pulmonologists were able to influence the choice of oxygen suppliers for patients needing oxygen at home.[46]

A similar antitrust issue may arise where a hospital, rather than a group of physicians, is the investor in the entity. If the hospital is the primary referror for certain types of services, then its involvement in a joint venture to which it also sends patients could raise antitrust issues. Several recent cases have now focused on the situation where a hospital forms a DME company to which patients being discharged from the hospital are referred.[47]

Advanced Health-Care Services v. Radford Community Hospital, in particular, illustrates a problem that can arise if one of the parties is a hospital that has a dominant share of the market. In that case, a DME supplier argued that two hospitals had entered into exclusive contracts with a rival DME supplier. Among the claims made were that the hospitals had market power in the provision of acute care hospital services, and that, as a result, the plaintiff DME company was being denied access to an essential facility controlled by the hospital; *i.e.*, patients being discharged from the hospitals.[48] While suppliers had previously been permitted access to these patients, this policy allegedly changed after the exclusive contract was effective. On remand, however, the District Court found that the plaintiff was not denied access to patients, and that access to the hospital's patients was not essential to doing business in the DME market.[49]

45. *See Arquit Speech*, at 13. *See also American Computech, Inc. v. National Medical Care, Inc.*, 1992 U.S. App. Lexis 6460 (9th Cir. 1992) (not-for-publication decision) (company made nephrologists medical directors at its dialysis centers).

46. *See* 58 Fed. Reg. at 60655.

47. *See Key Enterprises, Inc. v. Venice Hospital*, 703 F. Supp. 1513 (M.D. Fla. 1989), *rev'd* 919 F.2d 1550 (11th Cir. 1990), *vacated and rehearing en banc granted*, 979 F.2d 806 (11th Cir. 1992) *order granting en banc review vacated and appeal dismissed*, 9 F.3rd 893 (11th Cir. 1993); M&M *Medical Supplies and Service v. Pleasant Valley Hosp., Inc.*, 981 F.2d 160 (4th Cir. 1992) *cert. denied*, 113 S. Ct. 2962 (1993); *Advanced Health-Care Services v. Radford Comm. Hosp.*, 910 F.2d 139 (4th Cir. 1990), *on remand*, 846 F. Supp. 488 (W.D. Va. 1994) (granting summary judgment); *American Health Systems, Inc. v. Visiting Nurses Ass'n.*, 1994-1 Trade Cas. (CCH) ¶70,633 (E.D. Pa. 1994).

48. 910 F.2d at 150-51.

49. 846 F. Supp. at 498.

The primary way of dealing with the concerns that can be raised if the dominant hospital in the area participates in a joint venture is to ensure that patients are given a choice among other suppliers, or at least, are provided with information about such suppliers. In *Advanced Health Care,* for example, the hospital administrator: (1) advised patients requiring DME of all community suppliers; (2) refrained from recommending a supplier; and (3) required the patient to choose a supplier.[50] In one recent case, the state of Connecticut required a hospital that was integrating with a home health care agency to develop discharge procedures ensuring that patients were given information about the availability of similar services in their areas.[51]

2. *The Fraud and Abuse Issues*

In its Fraud Alert, the OIG expressed concern with joint ventures where the investors were chosen only because they were viewed as potential referrors. In the safe harbor regulation dealing with investment in small entities, five of the eight standards that must be met involve the issue of the selection of the venture participants.[52] These first five standards are set out below:

- No more than 40 percent of the investment interests may be held by investors who are in a position to generate business for the entity.

This provision prevents the entity from being composed largely of potential referrors. For purposes of this 40 percent test, those who provide items and services and those who refer patients to the entity are both considered "in a position to generate business" for the entity. In the preamble to the regulations, the OIG notes that this classification is necessary to preclude a supplier, such as a DME company, from forming a joint venture with referring physicians, by giving them a 39 percent interest. It would be inappropriate, according to the OIG, to grant safe harbor treatment to such a venture because all the owners would be doing business with the entity—either by supplying items and equipment to it or by making referrals to it.[53] For purposes of measuring the 40 percent standard, the OIG states the venture may use any internal accounting principles it chooses so long as they are used consistently. The time period for this measurement may be either over a previous 12-month period or over the prior fiscal year.[54]

50. *Id.*
51. *See* 62 Antitrust & Trade Reg. Rep. (BNA) 204 (Feb. 13, 1992).
52. 42 C.F.R. §1001.952(a)(2)(i)-(v).
53. 56 Fed. Reg. at 35,968.
54. *Id.* The OIG proposed some additional modifications to this provision in July, 1994. *See* 59 Fed. Reg. at 37204.

- The terms on which the investment interest is offered to a passive investor who is in a position to generate business for the entity must be no different than the terms offered to non-business generating passive investors.

The purpose of this standard is to ensure that an entity does not give referrors who invest in the entity more favorable terms than those who are not in a position to make such referrals. This standard does *not* apply to active investors, as the OIG concluded that active investors are often chosen because of their experience and may be offered special terms that are different than those offered to passive investors.[55] (As explained above, an active investor is either a general partner or someone who has undertaken liability for the entity's agents.)

- The terms on which the investment interest is offered to an investor who is in a position to generate business for the entity must not be related to the previous or expected volume of business generated by that investor for the entity.

This provision prevents an entity from offering more favorable terms to one investor merely because he or she has made referrals in the past or is expected to do so in the future. This standard applies to both active and passive investors.[56] Thus, this provision would prevent ventures from rewarding its largest referrors by offering them more favorable terms.

- There must be no requirement that a passive investor generate business for the entity as a condition for remaining an investor.

This provision prevents a venture from forcing investors to sell their shares back if they do not make referrals. This was an allegation in the *Hanlester* case.

- Neither the entity nor any investor may market or furnish the entity's items or services to passive investors differently than to non-investors.

The purpose of this requirement is to ensure that the entity promotes and furnishes items to investors and non-investors in the same manner. For example, the OIG notes, the entity can not use a separate marketing approach, or provide a different level of service, to investors, which is not available to non-investors.[57]

As noted above, if a venture fails to meet all the safe harbor requirements, it is not necessarily illegal. However, the general outlines discussed above should be followed as closely as possible. Finally, as the antikickback law only applies to Medicare and Medicaid referrals, if the venture did not accept such referrals, the provisions set out above would be inapplicable. State law might still apply, however.

55. *Id.*
56. *Id.*
57. *Id.*

3. *The Self-Referral Issues*

In many instances, it is the new self-referral provisions that will likely have the greatest impact on the selection of joint venture participants. Under Section 1877 of the Social Security Act, a physician cannot refer his or her Medicare or Medicaid patients "for designated services" to a facility in which he or she has an investment interest or with which he or she has a compensation arrangement, unless one of the enumerated exceptions applies. As a result, if this provision applies there may be little incentive for a venture to seek out potential referrors as investors.

Of course, a physician may still invest in such a venture, he or she simply may not refer any Medicare or Medicaid patients to the entity for these types of services specified in the law. A physician could still send non-Medicare and non-Medicaid patients to the facility, however, if there were no state self-referral law prohibiting such conduct. However, several of the health reform bills being considered by Congress would prohibit such referrals, regardless of who was paying for the services.

The Health Care Financing Administration ("HCFA") has proposed regulations interpreting the original self-referral provision, which applied only to laboratory services.[58] In many instances, these regulations would, if implemented, reach a broad range of activities engaged in by laboratories. When Congress amended the law in 1993, however, it effectively abrogated many of the provisions included in these proposed regulations.[59] Still, further changes may be made as a result of pending health care reform legislation.

Interestingly, under the current law, referrals by hospitals to affiliated entities are not covered by the self-referral provisions. Thus, the law does not prevent a hospital from referring its patients to an entity in which the hospital had an interest.[60] Under changes made by OBRA'93, however, referrals by physicians *to* a hospital may be prohibited, if the physician has an ownership interest or a compensation arrangement with the hospital.

58. 57 Fed. Reg. 8588 (Mar. 11, 1992). The OIG also issued proposed enforcement regulations. *See* 58 Fed. Reg. 54096 (Oct. 20, 1993).

59. For example, HCFA's proposed regulations defined "remuneration" to include "any payment, discount, foregiveness of debt or other benefit" flowing between the entity and the referror. This would have prohibited laboratories from giving physicians discounts on non-Medicare work, if the laboratory obtained the physician's Medicare or Medicaid testing. *See* 57 Fed. Reg. at 8594-95. In OBRA'93, Congress amended the law, however, so it was not considered remuneration when a physician paid a laboratory for clinical laboratory testing services. *See* 107 Stat. at 602.

60. Recently, however, the IRS has stated it will examine joint venture activities engaged in by non-profit hospitals to determine whether such ventures conflict with the hospital's tax-exempt purpose.

B. Structure of the Venture

1. *The Antitrust Issues*

The next significant issue to be considered is how the entity should be structured. As noted above, because joint ventures are often composed of entities or persons who are also competitors, the venture runs the risk of being condemned as an illegal combination violative of Section 1 of the Sherman Act. Thus, any agreement among the participants could raise antitrust concerns.

In *Arizona v. Maricopa County Medical Society*, the Supreme Court discussed the difference between an illegal combination of competitors and a legitimate joint venture.[61] In that case, the Supreme Court condemned a maximum fee schedule established by doctors participating in a local "Foundation for Medical Care." The Court distinguished the plan in that case from partnerships or joint ventures "in which persons who would otherwise be competitors pool their capital and share the risks of loss as well as the opportunities for profit. In such joint ventures, the partnership is regarded as a single firm competing with other sellers in the market."[62] In other situations, the Court has emphasized that joint ventures may make "possible a new product by reaping otherwise unattainable efficiencies."[63]

In structuring a joint venture, it will be necessary to ensure, at a minimum, that the teachings of *Maricopa* are met. This requirement should not be difficult in the usual case, so long as the venture is a legitimate entity to which the investors have contributed capital that is truly at risk. In some health care joint ventures, especially those established a number of years ago, investors did not actually put up any capital; rather they signed a note for their contribution, which was then repaid out of future profit distributions. The OIG raised concerns about such arrangements in its Fraud Alert and in the safe harbor regulations. Although such arrangements have not been tested under the antitrust laws, it could be argued that they were not legitimate joint ventures because the investor never put up his or her own capital, and was never truly at risk if the venture failed.

Even if the venture appears to meet the requirements of *Maricopa*, an additional antitrust issue could arise if the entity is "provider-controlled." In several cases, most of which involved physician-payor relationships, courts have looked to the composition of the board of directors of the entity and examined whether the entity was a combination of competitors who were using the particular plan as a shell by which to injure a rival.

61. 457 U.S. 332 (1982).
62. *Id.* at 356.
63. *NCAA v. Board of Regents of Univ. of Okla.*, 468 U.S. 85, 113 (1984).

For example, in *Virginia Academy of Clinical Psychologists v. Blue Shield of Virginia*,[64] the Fourth Circuit considered an antitrust challenge to a Blue Shield of Virginia policy, which precluded clinical psychologists from being reimbursed for their services unless they were billed through a physician. In that case the court found that the plan was controlled by competing physicians and that their action constituted concerted conduct violative of the Sherman Act.

Similarly, in *Hahn v. Oregon Physicians' Service*,[65] the Ninth Circuit condemned a preferred provider plan, which did not allow podiatrists to participate directly, and which reimbursed them on terms less favorable than those extended to competing physicians. In that case, the court reversed the lower court's grant of summary judgment because it found that the PPO's Board of Directors could be the agent of the competing physicians who controlled the Board. In that case, the court found, a jury might conclude that the physicians had used their control of the plan to reach agreements that worked to injure competing podiatrists.

While this theory does not appear to have been used to attack the types of joint venture being discussed here, in an appropriate case, it might be argued that a venture was actually controlled by competing providers who used it to injure competitors. This risk would be especially significant if the venture entered into ancillary agreements that served no obvious, procompetitive purpose, such as the billing restriction in *Virginia Academy*, discussed above.[66] One way to avoid this problem is to ensure that competing physicians do not constitute a majority of the board or to limit the number of physicians on the board through the by-laws. As an alternative, it should be clear that any ancillary agreements have some efficiency justification which can be demonstrated, if the arrangement is challenged.

2. *The Fraud and Abuse Issues*

As noted above, in its Fraud Alert the OIG stated its belief that the business structure of some joint ventures suggested an improper purpose. The OIG was especially concerned that the structure of the joint venture might be a shell, which was used to circumvent Medicare billing restrictions or was used to hide an illegal kickback.

64. 624 F.2d 476 (4th Cir. 1980).

65. 868 F.2d 1022 (9th Cir. 1988), *cert. denied*, 493 U.S. 846 (1989).

66. *See also, U.S. Healthcare, Inc. v. Healthsource, Inc.*, 986 F.2d 589, 594 (1st Cir. 1993) (argument that HMO's exclusivity provision was the result of a Board dominated by physicians, who wished to prevent entry by other HMOs, rejected for lack of evidence).

In the safe harbor regulations applicable to investment in small entities, the OIG expanded on its concern with the business structure of the operation. It included the following requirement specifically directed at the structure of the venture:[67]

- No more than 40 percent of the gross revenues of the entity may come from referrals or business generated from investors.

The preamble to the regulations states that the OIG did not believe entities should be able to exist simply by relying on the business that came from investing physicians.[68] Indeed the OIG noted that in many cases the referrals from investing physicians dominated the joint venture's business so that it did not have to compete for outside business. The purpose of the requirement set out above was to establish a "bright line" test which identified those ventures that relied too heavily on their investors for referrals. As with the other 60-40 rule, discussed above, the regulation permits the standard to be measured during a prior fiscal year or during a previous 12-month period.[69]

This provision is a difficult one for many entities to meet, and it is especially troublesome for new entities that do not yet have any referral experience to measure. The OIG does note, however, that it is unlikely to pursue an investigation of a venture that meets all the other standards, which is making a good faith effort to reach compliance with this standard. The OIG notes such good faith compliance can be shown from monthly reports, based on the most recent months of operation.[70]

One way of structuring the venture that avoids some of the fraud and abuse issues, and yet still allows the venture to obtain referrals from a key individual, is to make that person an employee of the venture. As noted earlier, the antikickback law states that a payment to an employee who has a bona fide employment relationship with an employer is not prohibited remuneration.[71]

The safe harbor regulations also include a provision that states that payments to employees are not remuneration for the purposes of the antikickback law.[72] Thus, so long as the individual meets the definition of an "employee" in the regulation, which is based on IRS regulations, payment to him or her should not

67. 42 C.F.R. §1001.952(a)(2)(vi). *See also* 59 Fed. Reg. at 37205 (proposed clarification of 60-40 rule).

68. 56 Fed Reg. at 35969.

69. *Id.*

70. *Id.*

71. Soc. Sec. Act, §1128B(b)(3)(B); 42 U.S.C. §1320a-7b(b)(3)(B).

72. 42 C.F.R. §1001.952(i).

implicate the antikickback law in most cases.[73] Independent contractors, however, are *not* covered by this safe harbor.

The OIG has recently made some public statements that indicate a desire to restrict the employee safe harbor, and has expressed particular concern about large bonus payments made to employees based on the volume of ancillary services that they order. For example, in one instance cited by the OIG, employees were paid 30 percent of the gross billings of the ancillary services for which they referred patients, an arrangement that gives the physicians an obvious incentive to increase referrals. While the OIG has stated that such arrangements are not payment for employment, and thus may not be covered by the employee safe harbor, that argument seems a difficult one for the OIG to make given the broad language of the safe harbors.[74] Several of the health reform bills currently being considered by Congress, however, would basically prohibit payments to employees that varied with the value of referrals, a provision that would eliminate the sorts of arrangements described above. The bills would permit the payment of "productivity bonuses" for services actually rendered by the employee, however.

Another issue related to the employment safe harbor has been the subject of some controversy as a result of recent public statements by D. McCarty Thornton, the Chief Counsel of the Inspector General Division of the HHS Office of General Counsel. In a widely discussed letter to T.J. Sullivan of the IRS, dated December 22, 1992, Mr. Thornton responded to a request from the IRS for an opinion on an arrangement where a professional medical association sold its tangible and intangible assets to a hospital or multihospital network. Under the arrangement, the physicians then became employees of the network. In his letter, Thornton stated that payment for intangible assets, such as goodwill, value of a going concern, covenants not to compete, exclusive dealing contracts, and patient and physician lists, would raise issues under the antikickback law. According to Thornton's letter, payments in excess of the value of the tangible assets could be construed as payments for future referrals by the physician-employees.

While Thornton has backed off from his letter somewhat,[75] it does raise a significant concern for entities that are purchasing on-going businesses and paying for "goodwill" or similar intangible assets. The OIG was reportedly

73. One problem with making such individuals employees may be state "corporate practice of medicine" laws, which may prevent a corporation from employing a physician in this way. *See* 56 Fed. Reg. at 35,981-82.

74. *See* "HHS Official Tempers Agency Hardline on Acquisition of Physician Practices," 4 BNA's Medicare Rep. 394 (April 2, 1993) (hereinafter "*BNA Med. Rep.*").

75. *See BNA Med. Rep., supra.*

considering issuing some guidance in this area, but to date it has not been forthcoming. Interestingly, the OIG's letter was spawned by an inquiry from the IRS, which was considering the purchaser's request for tax-exempt status. As a result of the OIG's letter, the IRS granted the exemption but stated the approval was conditioned on the arrangement not violating the fraud and abuse laws, an issue on which it expressed no opinion.[76]

3. *The Self-Referral Issues*

The major structural concerns raised by the self-referral law usually revolve around the particular exceptions set out in the law. Ventures will obviously try to choose a structure that allows them to qualify for one of these exceptions. Although there is no "small entity" exception comparable to that in the safe harbor regulations, there is an exception for large publicly traded entities. This exception is similar, but not identical, to the safe harbor provision for publicly traded entities.[77] Thus, larger entities that qualify under this exemption will be able to accept referrals from their investors.

A second major exemption involves group practices. Under the self-referral law, a facility owned by a group practice is permitted to accept referrals from its member-physicians, without violating the law, provided the requirements set out in the statute are met. The self-referral law, as amended by OBRA'93, included six different requirements that must be met for a practice to qualify as a group practice. In essence, this provision requires group members to provide their services through joint use of shared office space, facilities and personnel; to bill through the group; and to share income and overhead expenses. In addition, members of the group must personally conduct no less than 75 percent of the patient encounters of the group. Finally, members of the group cannot be paid based on the volume or value of their referrals, although they may be paid bonuses based on the overall profits of the group or on the services that they perform.[78]

To take advantage of this exception, some physician-owned entities restructured to become "group practices without walls." Under this scenario, individual physicians with their own practices form a group practice, though each physician keeps his or her own office location. The "group practice" will also furnish

76. *See* Facey Med. Foundation, 93 Tax Notes Today 83-116 (Apr. 15, 1993).

77. For example, the self-referral law states that to qualify for its exemption, the entity must have $100 million in "total assets," as opposed to $50 million in "net undepreciated tangible assets," which is required by the safe harbor regulations. OBRA'93 changed the $100 million total asset requirement to require companies to have $75 million in "shareholder equity," beginning in 1995, if they are to qualify for the exemption in the self-referral law.

78. OBRA '93, §13562(h)(4), 107 Stat. at 603.

ancillary services to which the members refer patients. While there may be some minimal sharing of expenses, often each physician is allowed to keep the share of the revenues that he or she generates, including the revenues from the ancillary services. Thus, in many instances, the group practice actually functions much as an ancillary service joint venture.

If the arrangement can qualify as a group practice, referrals to the laboratory would be exempt if all the applicable requirements are met.[79] However, it may be more difficult for such ventures to meet the requirements for a group, established by OBRA'93. Several of the health reform bills are trying to further limit these arrangements by requiring greater integration of the group practice.

Finally, while the self-referral law did not initially contain an exemption for referrals from a physician-employee to his or her employer, when the law was amended by OBRA'93, an explicit exemption was included for employment arrangements, although certain specific requirements must still be met.[80] In this way, the self-referral law was made consistent with the antikickback law and the safe harbor provisions.[81]

C. Financing and Profit Distributions

1. *The Antitrust Issues*

In most instances, the way an entity distributes profits or revenues to its partners or investors, is unlikely to raise antitrust issues.[82] In one case, a court recently concluded that a hospital's agreement to pay physicians who referred patients to the hospital did not violate the antitrust laws because there was no allegation that the hospital had market power in any relevant market.[83]

In other cases, however, the courts have noted that particular forms of distributions between an entity and those who refer to it could constitute predatory conduct, one of the requirements for a claim of monopolization or attempted monopolization.[84] For example, in *Advanced Health-Care Service v. Radford Comm. Hosp.*,[85] the plaintiff alleged that the hospitals paid their

79. Soc. Sec. Act, §1877(b)(2); 42 U.S.C. §1395nn(b)(2).

80. OBRA '93, §13562(e)(2), 107 Stat. at 599.

81. For antitrust purposes, a contract between an employee and an employer would usually not be a violation of Section 1 of the Sherman Act, as there would not be two separate entities. *See Copperweld Corp. v. Independence Tube Corp.*, 467 U.S. 752, 769 (1984).

82. *E.g.*, Letter to Gilbert M. Frimet from Arthur N. Lerner, Ass't. Director, FTC Bureau of Competition, (Mar. 22, 1984) (use of a fee schedule to distribute revenues to IPA members unlikely to create antitrust concerns).

83. *Health First v. Bronson Methodist Hosp.*, 1990-2 Trade Cas. (CCH) ¶69200 (W.D. Mi. 1990).

84. *E.g.*, *Aspen Skiing Co. v. Aspen Highlands Skiing Corp.*, 472 U.S. 585 (1985).

85. 910 F.2d 139 (4th Cir. 1990).

discharge personnel $40 for each patient ordering equipment from the affiliated DME supplier. In reversing the district court's grant of summary judgment, the court of appeals noted that the hospital's payment scheme could suggest an anticompetitive motive on the part of the hospital. The court also required some evidence that the quality of the DME provided in the market had gone down, or that the price had increased.[86] On remand, however, the District Court found no evidence to support these allegations and granted summary judgment for the defendant hospital.[87]

Another case, *American Computech v. National Medical Care*,[88] raised similar issues. In that case West Coast, a supplier of dialysis services sued a rival provider and the physicians with whom it contracted. The defendant, National Medical Care ("NMC"), contracted with doctors to act as medical directors at its dialysis facilities. The doctors were then paid a percentage of the net profits generated by these facilities. These arrangements allegedly gave the company an advantage in obtaining hospital business, because these physicians were often involved in the selection of a dialysis provider. The court stated that the fact that the physicians were paid a percentage of earnings could suggest an anticompetitive intent on the part of NMC. According to the court, "Because the doctors received fifty percent of NMC's earnings in providing hospitals with dialysis services, West Coast argued to the jury that this financial incentive was designed by NMC to keep the doctors from competing with NMC and to impair their neutrality in recommending a dialysis provider."[89] The court found this arrangement demonstrated an intent to injure competition.

Similarly, the court also found that the company's specific intent to monopolize was shown by the fact that it "attempted to retain the doctors' services as medical directors by offering them high compensation for minimal work in an attempt to maintain the high level of referrals to its facilities and thereby abolish West Coast as a competitor and regain their ability to dictate price."[90] Thus, there is some suggestion that agreements that give referrors a percentage of their own referrals, which would likely constitute a kickback under the fraud and abuse laws, can constitute a violation of the antitrust laws, at least when the entity has market power.[91]

86. *Id.* at 148.

87. 846 F.Supp. at 493-95. *See also, American Health Systems v. Visiting Nurses Ass'n.*, 1994 Trade Cas. (CCH) ¶70,633 (allegations that home health agency made illegal kickbacks to hospitals in exchange for referrals).

88. 1992 U.S. App. Lexis 6460 (9th Cir. 1992) (not-for-publication decision).

89. *Id.* at 9.

90. *Id.* at 15.

91. *But see Pacifica Kidney Center v. National Medical Care*, 1993 U.S. App. Lexis 13536 (9th Cir. 1993) (not-for-publication decision) (court dismisses attack on an agreement comparable to the one at issue in *Computech*). Such contracts could also violate Section 2(c) of the Robinson-Patman Act.

2. *The Fraud and Abuse Issues*

It is in this area of payment that the antikickback law is most directly implicated. A direct payment by a provider to a referror in exchange for Medicare or Medicaid business would constitute an illegal kickback.[92] As discussed above, the *Greber* case involved a company that "rebated" 40 percent of the amount it received from Medicare back to the referring physician, action which the court found illegal.[93] Thus, the payments alleged in *Advanced Health Care* or *Computech* might very well constitute violations of the antikickback law. However, because there is currently no private right of action under the antikickback law, injured competitors who lose business cannot sue for such violations.

The safe harbors also include two requirements relevant to financing and profit distributions.[94] These are:

- The entity must not loan funds to or guarantee a loan for an investor who is in a position to generate business for the entity.

This standard was added to ensure that the investor actually put his or her own funds at risk. As discussed above, the OIG had found that in other situations, the investor never actually put up any cash; he or she simply borrowed from the entity and that loan was then repaid out of future distributions. Under the clarification recently issued by the OIG, other *investors* would also be prohibited from making such loans.[95]

- The profits distributed to an investor must be directly proportional to the amount of the capital investment.

The purpose of this provision is to ensure that payments reflect the interest owned by the investor. The payments cannot disguise payments for referrals. As noted above, to qualify for safe harbor treatment, all eight of the standards set out above must be met. If an entity does not comply, then its payments are not protected.

A related issue has arisen in the context of payments by managed care plans to participating physicians. In many instances, such plans give participating physicians financial incentives to reduce or limit utilization. For example, most common are "withholds," a percentage of payments or set dollar amounts that the plan deducts from each physician's payment. If the HMO's costs for certain

92. *See United States v. Weingarden*, 468 F.Supp. 410, 412-13 (E.D. Mich. 1979), *aff'd sub nom., United States v. Hancock*, 604 F.2d 999 (7th Cir. 1979), *cert. denied*, 444 U.S. 991 (1991).

93. 760 F.2d at 68-69.

94. 42 C.F.R. §952(a)(2)(vii)-(viii).

95. *See* 59 Fed. Reg. at 37204.

services exceeds an amount budgeted, then the withhold may be forfeited; otherwise, it is divided among the participating physicians. Because of concerns that such physician incentive plans might result in enrollees not obtaining medically necessary services, the OIG has proposed standards to govern such arrangements.[96]

3. *The Self-Referral Issues*

The self-referral law does not have a direct impact on the financing or profit distribution of the entity. However, as most exemptions in the law require that payments not vary with the volume or value of referrals, the law could still affect how referrors are paid for various services that they legitimately provide to the entity, such as consulting services or interpreting x-rays or test results. This requirement is designed to ensure that payments do not disguise unlawful rewards for referrals.

There is one instance in which payments are permitted to vary with the volume or value of referrals. This is in the case of "physician incentive plans," such as withhold payments discussed above. Because such payments reward physicians for reducing or limiting their referrals, they *do* vary with referrals. The self-referral law is primarily concerned, however, with instances—unlike these arrangements—where referrors *increase* their referrals in response to financial incentives. Because incentives to reduce utilization were not the concern of the law, Congress added an exemption for physician incentive plans that meet certain requirements, when it amended the law as part of OBRA'93.[97]

There is one other significant issue that arises in the financing of the venture under the self-referral law. After the initial self-referral law applicable only to laboratories was passed, many ventures purchased equipment or facilities from physician-owned laboratory entities. Where possible, the new entity would obviously want to continue to obtain the referrals of the former owners. One method of "locking-in" the past owners was to make the purchase payments on an installment basis, thereby giving the previous owners a continued interest in the success of the venture. In its proposed regulations, which would have applied only to laboratory services, HCFA took the position that the entity would have a continuing financial relationship with the former owners until all payments were completed. HCFA noted that physicians receiving such installment payments "would retain an incentive to refer business to the laboratory to maintain the financial validity of the laboratory."[98] As a result, under this view,

96. *See* 57 Fed. Reg. at 59024 (Dec. 14, 1992).
97. *See* OBRA '93, §13562(e)(3)(B), 107 Stat. at 600.
98. 57 Fed. Reg. at 8596.

the entity could not accept referrals from the physicians until the debt was paid off.

III. GUIDELINES FOR THE OPERATION OF JOINT VENTURES

After the venture is formed, and is actually in operation, some issues may arise that are not addressed by the framework discussed above. While many such issues could arise in any health care venture, we will address three key issues in this article. They are: (1) steering or "channeling" patients to the venture; (2) discouraging referrors from using other providers; and (3) issues related to pricing the services of the venture. The discussion will focus primarily on issues that arise when referrors are also investors in the entity, although much of the analysis will be applicable to any health care joint venture.

A. "Channeling" Patients to the Venture

1. *The Antitrust Issues*

In general, joint ventures may wish to impose two related types of restrictions on their referrors. In some instances, ventures may try to require providers to refer only to the joint venture, which is basically what is referred to as "channeling." As an alternative, the venture may try to effect the same goal indirectly, by discouraging or prohibiting providers from referring to other competing providers. In either event, from an antitrust viewpoint, the essential question is the same: what is the impact on competition among the firms providing the same services as the joint venture? Are they able to obtain the referrals that they need to survive?

First, we will turn to the question of channeling—the explicit steering of patients to an ancillary services joint venture by providers who have an investment interest in the entity. For example, could a physician be required to refer his or her patients to the entity in which he or she has invested? Or, could a hospital agree to refer its patients to a DME venture in which the hospital has an interest? While much of the discussion above touched on issues related to channeling, this section will deal directly with the practice.

In his article discussed above, the FTC's Mark Horoschak noted that an agreement, either express or implied, to refer patients to an entity in which the referror has an interest could raise issues under Section 1 of the Sherman Act, and that such issues would usually be assessed under the rule of reason. He noted: "The anticompetitive effect of the agreement would depend both on the nature of the restraint—limiting referrals to the jointly-owned venture—and the proportion of potential referring physicians represented by the group entering this undertaking."[99] In short, if there were an agreement to refer, and the proportion of physicians involved in the entity was so great that other firms were unlikely to enter the market served by the venture, then a rule of reason violation could be found.

As Mr. Horoschak notes, the essential question here is this: What is the impact on other firms providing the same services as those supplied by the group venture.[100] Given that providers who invest in such facilities are more likely to utilize those facilities, it could be argued that such arrangements do indeed make it more difficult for other providers, without such investor-referrors, to compete. Such an impact may be especially likely with health care ventures, because most patients lack detailed knowledge about health care services and are unable to judge among competing providers. Moreover, because of the physicians' investment interests, it may be more difficult for other competitors to obtain these physicians' referrals through competition on the merits.

The Supreme Court's recent decision in *Eastman Kodak v. Image Technical Services*,[101] suggests that such an argument should be seriously considered. In that case, it was alleged that Kodak, which manufactured copying equipment, would only sell replacement parts to buyers of Kodak equipment who used Kodak service or who repaired their own machines, thus restricting competition from independent service organizations. Kodak argued that its actions could not constitute an illegal tying agreement, whereby Kodak parts were tied to Kodak service, unless it had market power in the equipment market. Kodak argued that if it attempted to exercise market power in the parts and service market, consumers would simply purchase other equipment with better service terms.[102]

In rejecting this argument, the Court emphasized that it had to "examine[] closely the economic reality of the market at issue."[103] It found Kodak's theory unconvincing because there were significant information and switching costs in the market; that is, to understand the impact of a price increase in the service market, consumers purchasing the equipment would have to inform themselves of the entire package cost over the life of the equipment, a difficult and costly process. Second, given the initial cost of the equipment, it would be difficult for consumers to easily switch to different equipment should service costs increase. Furthermore, according to the Court, there was evidence that Kodak had

99. *Horoschak* at 6.

100. *See also, Action Ambulance Service v. Atlanticare Health Services*, 815 F.Supp. 33 (D. Mass. 1993) (contract requiring hospital to refer all patients in need of ambulance services to defendant in exchange for 50 percent of profits, could constitute illegal tying arrangement).

101. 112 S.Ct. 2072 (1992).

102. *Id.* at 2081-82.

103. *Id.* at 2082.

increased prices and excluded competition. As a result, the Court determined that summary judgment for Kodak was improper.

The *Kodak* decision has significant implications for health care joint ventures, given its emphasis on actual market conditions rather than theoretical constructs. After *Kodak*, it may be easier to argue that joint ventures composed of a large proportion of potential referrors, are anticompetitive, under a rule of reason analysis. A competitor attacking the venture would likely argue that the venture was able to exercise market power, because most patients cannot make price and service comparisons. In addition, such a competitor would also argue that it was unable to attract patients, because many of the potential referrors were unwilling to refer to another entity in which they do not have an interest. As a result, *Kodak* suggests that courts may be more willing to condemn ventures that have engaged in some form of channeling. It may also be necessary to show, however, some actual impact on competition, such as increased prices or excluded competition.[104]

In addition to examining these claims under Section 1, courts have also examined such cases under Section 2 of the Sherman Act, which prohibits monopolization and attempted monopolization. In these cases, it is alleged that the practice of channeling allows the entity to monopolize the market occupied by the joint venture. In *M&M Medical Supplies and Service v. Pleasant Valley Hospital*,[105] a DME supplier sued a hospital and its DME subsidiary for monopolization, attempted monopolization and conspiracy to monopolize. In vacating the district court's grant of summary judgment, the court concluded the following actions were supportive of a monopolization claim: a memorandum had been sent to physicians practicing at the hospital suggesting they use the DME company affiliated with the hospital; one patient was specifically told that only the hospital's company could supply the equipment; hospital regulations were changed to prohibit the use of equipment from outside vendors; in several instances, the hospital ordered equipment for patients without consulting them or telling them they had a choice of providers; and, finally, the hospital's DME affiliate had raised prices above those of its rival, without losing business.[106]

As discussed above, the best way to avoid such problems is either to give patients information about rival companies or, at the very least, to ensure that

104. *But see Pacifica Kidney Ctr. v. National Medical Care*, 1193 U.S. App. Lexis 13536 at 8 (9th Cir. 1993) (court rejects an argument that channeling by itself is illegal). *See also Advanced Health Care*, 846 F.Supp. 488 (on remand).

105. 981 F.2d 160 (4th Cir. 1992), *cert. denied*, 113 S.Ct. 2962 (1993).

106. *Id.* at 167. *But see, Advanced Health Care*, 846 F.Supp. at 495 (rejecting monopolization claim because there was no evidence to support the argument that hospital had exercised monopoly power).

they understand they have a choice of suppliers. Moreover, pricing actions that could be evidence of market power should be carefully weighed. In addition, memoranda, such as those in *M&M* which urge physicians to use the affiliated company, should be avoided.

2. *The Fraud and Abuse Issues*

If some form of remuneration were given to physicians in exchange for their agreement to refer all their patients to the payor, the OIG would be likely to argue that the fraud and abuse laws were violated. In fact, the safe harbors specifically state that no immunity will be afforded to entities if investors are required to refer as a condition of the investment.[107]

Similarly, if the venture actively encourages investors to make such referrals to it, then it could appear that any payments made as a return on investment constituted remuneration to induce referrals. For example, in *Hanlester*, prospective investors were told it would be a "blueprint for failure" if the parties did not refer to the entity. Even tracking each investor's referrals, and informing him or her of the results, could raise issues under the fraud and abuse laws. Similarly, dividend payments that are proportional to the amount of referrals would also be considered remuneration for referrals. This was one factor that the ALJ in *Hanlester* was directed to consider in making his determination of whether the ventures were unlawful. Such payments are also prohibited under the safe harbors.

A related issue arises in this area when one health care provider agrees to give a discount to a managed care plan or other payor in exchange for an agreement that the managed care plan will refer patients to the provider. At least if the plan's enrollees were Medicare patients, it could be argued that such a discount constituted remuneration given in exchange for referrals, and thus violated the antikickback law. As noted above, the OIG issued a second set of safe harbor provisions that address when such discounts will be immunized.[108]

3. *The Self-Referral Issues*

As the self-referral laws make it unlawful for a physician to refer to an entity with which he or she has a financial relationship, requiring an investor to refer

107. 42 C.F.R. §1000.952(a)(2)(iv).

108. *See* 56 Fed. Reg. at 52723 (Nov. 5, 1992). In addition, as noted above, the OIG has proposed regulations that will apply to the physician incentive plans used by many managed care plans. 57 Fed. Reg. at 59024 (Dec. 14, 1992).

to the entity is directly prohibited by these laws. Moreover, as the self-referral law applies whenever there is a compensation arrangement between a referror and an entity, it will prohibit "channeling" in many situations in which the referror is not actually an investor in the entity.[109]

B. Discouraging Referrors from Using Other Providers

1. *The Antitrust Issues*

In some instances, a venture may not explicitly require its investors to refer to it, but it may discourage them from using other competitors. In the health care area, antitrust cases have often closely scrutinized such agreements. For example, in *Blue Cross of Washington v. Kitsap Physicians Service*,[110] the court condemned a provision in the by-laws of an HMO that prohibited members from participating in other HMOs. Given Kitsap's position as the dominant insurer in the area, the court held the likely effect of the provision would be to deny new entrants access to the physicians needed to operate.[111] Similarly, in his speech discussed above, then-Assistant Attorney General James Rill stated that in the PPO context, exclusivity arrangements can be anticompetitive if "they exclude competing delivery systems and significantly constrict fee-for-service options."[112] In the "Antitrust Policy Statements," the FTC and the Department of Justice note that non-exclusive arrangements may pose substantially less risk than exclusive arrangements.[113]

In another situation, the FTC refused to approve an HMO plan that discouraged physician-members from owning shares of a competing HMO. Physicians who invested in such competing plans were to be given a different class of stock, with reduced rights, than other physicians. Given the large percentage of physicians in the area who were members of the HMO, the FTC determined that the proposed limitation could make it difficult for new HMOs to gain access to the physicians they were likely to need to compete successfully.[114]

109. As noted, however, Congress did add an exemption for "physician incentive plans" used by managed care plans in OBRA '93.

110. 1982-1 Trade Cas. (CCH) ¶64,588 (W.D. Wash. 1982).

111. *Id. See also Potters Med. Ctr. v. City Hosp. Ass'n.*, 800 F.2d 568 (6th Cir. 1986) (tactics by a dominant hospital to keep physicians from seeking staff privileges or referring other work to rival hospital could constitute monopolization).

112. *See Rill Speech*, note 42, *supra*.

113. 4 Trade Reg. Rep. ¶13,150 at 20,765.

114. Letter to Gilbert M. Frimet from Arthur N. Lerner, Ass't Director, FTC Bureau of Competition (Mar. 22, 1984).

Recently, however, the First Circuit analyzed a similar arrangement and found, at least, that it was not *per se* illegal. In *U.S. Healthcare, Inc. v. Healthsource, Inc.*,[115] an HMO paid its physicians a higher capitation payment if they agreed not to participate in any other HMO plan, though they could still participate in other indemnity plans. Originally, doctors had to give 180 days notice before terminating this agreement, though this was later shortened to 30 days. The court rejected a rival HMO's argument that such an arrangement was *per se* illegal. There was insufficient evidence in the record to allow an analysis under the rule of reason. The court did hint, however, that a termination provision requiring 180 days' notice might be problematic, because it would make it more difficult for new competitors to obtain the necessary physician contracts. However, there was insufficient evidence in the record to allow it to make a final determination.

In sum, agreements that limit referrors—either by promoting channeling or discouraging the use of other providers—must be closely examined in light of market conditions to determine their legality under the antitrust laws.

2. *The Fraud and Abuse Issues*

There are no specific provisions that deal with the status of discouraging referrals to competing ventures in the fraud and abuse laws. However, it seems likely that such activities would be analyzed much as explicit channeling; *i.e.*, as a requirement that all referrals be made to the entity. In *Hanlester*, as discussed above, physicians were strongly encouraged to refer to the venture, a factor that was important in the determination that the arrangement violated the fraud and abuse laws.

3. *The Self-Referral Issues*

As noted, it is the practice of channeling that is prohibited by the self-referral laws. Therefore, those providers that have a financial relationship with an entity will be unable to refer to it; thus, discouraging them from using another entity will probably not arise as an issue.

C. Pricing of the Ventures/Services

1. *The Antitrust Issues*

Issues involving price are the most sensitive under the antitrust laws. An ancillary service joint venture, such as we are discussing here, presents two

115. 986 F.2d 589 (1st Cir. 1993).

primary pricing issues. First, can the price for the venture's services be set without violating the antitrust laws? Second, is there a risk of "spillover" collusion?

As noted above, many of those involved in the joint venture are likely to be competitors in their usual practices. Thus, an agreement on how to price the services of the joint venture, could raise questions of price-fixing. If the venture meets the requirements of *Maricopa* set out above, however, then the venture is permitted to set a price for its services. As noted above, *Maricopa* required some minimal level of integration and some sharing of risk. In other situations where such integration was found, the Court has noted a consequence of the operation of the venture is that a price for its services must be established.[116] In most ancillary service joint ventures, the requirements of *Maricopa* are likely to be met; *i.e.*, there is sufficient integration and risk sharing to qualify as a legitimate joint venture. Thus, under the cases cited above, setting the price for the venture's services will not constitute price fixing.[117]

In addition, the second risk in this area is "spillover" collusion, *i.e.* an agreement among the investors on competitively sensitive terms relevant to their own practices. Thus, if all the investors in the entity were physicians, care should be taken that they do not exchange sensitive information that could affect competition in their own product markets, rather than the markets occupied by the joint venture.

2. *The Fraud and Abuse Issues*

Pricing of the services of the health care joint venture can create special issues under the fraud and abuse laws. First, as noted above, the investors, or those who generate business for the entity, cannot be given special pricing considerations on the services of the entity, nor can the services of the joint venture be marketed differently to such investors. The safe harbor provisions specifically state that investors in the entity cannot be given special prices or other consideration not available to non-investors.[118]

In addition, as noted above, special concerns can arise under the fraud and abuse laws where the seller gives a discount to the buyer, at least where the services subject to the discount will be reimbursed by Medicare or Medicaid.

116. *See Broadcast Music, Inc. v. Columbia Broadcasting System, Inc.*, 441 U.S. 1, 21 (1979). *See also Hassan v. Independent Practice Assoc.*, 698 F.Supp. 679 (E.D. Mich. 1998).

117. For a fuller discussion of the pricing issues created by joint ventures, see K. Grady, *A Framework for Antitrust Analysis of Health Care Joint Ventures*, 61 Antitrust L.J. 765 (1993).

118. *See* 42 C.F.R. §1001.952(a)(2)(v).

Under the antikickback law, the definition of "remuneration" specifically excludes discounts or other reductions in price if the reduction in price is properly disclosed and appropriately reflected in the costs claimed or charges made.[119] In the safe harbor provisions, the OIG established a special provision for discounts.[120] Under that provision, a discount is not remuneration in most instances, so long as the buyer reports the amount of the discount of either its cost reports or when filing claims. The seller is required to notify the buyer of the value of the discount and the buyer's obligation to report that amount when seeking payment from Medicare. The OIG defines discount as a reduction in the amount a seller charges a buyer for a good or service based on an arms' length transaction. However, several types of transactions are specifically excluded from the definition of discounts, including the following: (1) cash payment; (2) furnishing one good or service without charge or at a low price in exchange for any agreement to buy a different item or service; (3) a reduction applicable to one payor but not to Medicare or Medicaid; or (4) a reduction in price offered to a beneficiary, such as a routine waiver of coinsurance.

3. *The Self-Referral Laws*

Similar types of issues can arise under the self-referral law as arise under the fraud and abuse laws. For example, as noted above, a compensation arrangement is created whenever there is "remuneration" that flows between a referror and a joint venture.[121] Under the first set of regulations proposed to implement the self-referral law, which only applied to laboratory services, the term "remuneration" was broadly defined to include "any payment, discount, forgiveness of debt or other benefit" that flows between the entity and the referror. This meant that whenever an entity sold services at a discount to a referror, a compensation arrangement could be created.[122] As noted above, this provision was essentially abrogated by OBRA'93; however, revisions contained in one of the health reform bills would require the services to be provided at fair market value.

IV. PUTTING IT ALL TOGETHER

As the above discussion demonstrates, it will be more and more difficult for providers to form joint ventures if they also wish to refer to them or otherwise do business with them. However, in forming and operating such a venture, here are a few specific guidelines to consider.

119. Soc. Sec. Act, 1128B(b)(3); 42 U.S.C. §1320a-7b(b)(3).
120. 42 C.F.R. §1001.952(h).
121. Soc. Sec. Act, §1877(h); 42 U.S.C. §1395nn(h).
122. 57 Fed. Reg. at 8588.

1. Consider the self-referral laws first. In most instances, it will be the self-referral laws that will most limit the activities of the joint venture. Therefore, begin with an examination of the federal and state self-referral laws to determine whether they will have an impact on who will be able to refer to the venture. Examine the various exceptions to see if any of them is applicable to the venture.

2. After the self-referral law is considered, then consider the fraud and abuse laws, because they also will be severely limiting. In reviewing the fraud and abuse implications, consider the following:

- Review the safe harbor regulations. Even if the venture cannot comply with all of the applicable requirements, try to comply with as many as possible, as closely as possible.
- Watch, in particular, for any agreements that fluctuate with the volume and value of referrals; *e.g.*, contracts that give referrors a percentage of the revenue created by their referrals.
- Ensure that the venture is not composed entirely or largely of referrors.
- Avoid having the venture (or other investors) make loans to investor-referrors, especially if the funds are to be used to purchase an interest in the entity.
- Remember that virtually any benefit provided to referrors by the entity could be considered "remuneration," under the antikickback law. If such payments are necessary, ensure that they comply with the applicable safe harbor.
- Avoid requirements that the investor refer patients to the particular entity in which he or she has an interest.
- Consider making key individuals employees or active investors, rather than passive investors.
- Finally, remember that many states also have their own antikickback laws, so be sure that the requirements of those laws are also considered.

3. Finally, consider the antitrust laws, which are likely to be the least restrictive of the three sets of laws discussed here.

- Ensure that no more than 30-35 percent of the likely referrors in the market are involved in the venture.
- If the dominant hospital in the area is involved in the venture, ensure that patients are given information about rival providers of the service and ensure that they understand they have a choice among providers.
- Avoid memoranda or other materials that discourage physicians from using other providers or that encourage them to use the joint venture facilities.

- Ensure that the venture meets the requirements of *Maricopa; i.e.*, there must be some integration of activities and sharing of risk.
- Consider carefully any ancillary agreements to ensure that they are reasonably necessary to the purposes of the venture. In particular, scrutinize closely any arrangement that requires physicians to use the services of the venture or prohibits them from using other providers.
- Ensure that there is no "spillover collusion;" *i.e.*, that the providers are not exchanging sensitive information not involved in the joint venture.

With this background, it will be easier to avoid any of the obvious pitfalls that await such ventures.

9 780834 207110

Printed in Dunstable, United Kingdom

91338349R00029